The Sea and Me

Stories of My Scuba Diving Adventures

Leonor Osorio Granado

THE SEA AND ME: STORIES OF MY SCUBA DIVING ADVENTURES

First edition. April 29, 2024.

ISBN: 979-8224240616

Written by LEONOR OSORIO GRANADO.

Table of Contents

Dedication

I dedicate this book to the memory of my parents for instilling in me a great sense of responsibility, discipline, and respect. To my sisters and brothers, for always enthusiastically supporting my ideas and initiatives. To my daughters Ailyn and Aldys and sons-in-law, for their unconditional support, their constant love, and their contribution in technical matters of this project, and finally to my granddaughters Mia and Alba, hoping that they find in my stories the necessary inspiration and the correct path, which take them to fulfill their dreams and perhaps one day, we can immerse ourselves together in the wonderful underwater world.

Thanks

I wish to thank my friends and scuba diving instructors: Alfredo Chirinos, Arturo Chirinos, Roberto Borges and Wladimir A. Garcia, who constantly shared with me their scuba diving knowledge in a generous way.

My Passion for the Sea

More than 70% of the surface of our beautiful planet is covered by oceans and seas. However, this world under the oceans and seas is not available to everyone.

We can see it in videos, movies, and books, but the vast majority do not know in person what this aquatic world houses. Even those who have ventured into scuba diving barely know a fraction of the immensity of the sea.

From a very young age I discovered that my love for the sea was really a passion for knowing and enjoying that underwater world.

I didn't imagine what could be in such immensity. The idea that there were animals of different shapes and colors came to my childhood mind, but I never imagined that the seabed houses so much flora, fauna and so much beauty.

As a child, going to the beach with my family was one of my favorite things. My brothers, sisters and I played near the shore and, with the water up to our waists, with the help of a children's mask, we could see, very close to our feet, some pebbles, seashells, some small fish and sometimes algae.

There was always the curiosity to know what was in the deepest part of the beach, where the sea takes on a darker tone, but going into the depths was forbidden to me because "it was dangerous and I had to learn how to swim first and defend myself from the waves.", before going there.

My curiosity to know about that underwater world filled my head with fantasies and thousands of ideas fluttered in me: "One day I would have the joy of diving beyond the shore, where my feet would no longer be able to touch the bottom....Yes, someday I would have to know and discover what is there under those dark blue waters"

During my teenage years I had the joy of living in Macuto, a coastal city, near Caracas, Venezuela. The sea was very close to our house, maybe a couple of blocks, and I remember that at night you could hear the waves breaking on the shore of the beach. That sound was lulling and relaxing to me.

Given the proximity to the sea, we spent part of each Saturday at the beach. We enjoyed every moment of its fresh breeze and its clear, warm waters.

Especially in the hottest months, we knew that a plunge into the sea could make anyone's day.

On weekdays, we had to walk to school. and that walk was short and very pleasant, because the journey was almost entirely along a sidewalk that bordered the coast.

These walks were pleasant and relaxing for me, my eyes would get lost in the distance to the ocean trying to see if a dolphin or a fishing boat appeared. I was always amazed by the force with which the waves hit the rocks on the shore of the pier, leaving trails with its foam, which I gave shapes to in my mind, but which quickly vanished when the water returned.

I think it was at this time in my life when my love for the sea really began. Not touching the bottom of the sea with my feet, at first was shocking, but little by little I adapted to floating in its waters and started to gain more confidence in myself as a swimmer.

As I learned how to swim, I started to get far, towards the buoy, trying to experience a wonderful new challenge, and enjoying every minute of it.

My dad constantly dared us to swim farther, but always with him.

I learned the importance of respecting the sea, because I knew that the waves and underlying currents could give us a good scare. Therefore, when we moved away from the shore, it was important to go with an experienced swimmer, and that swimmer was my dad.

We were a family of eight: six children, plus my parents, and we all loved going to the beach. Enjoying those days by the sea and becoming familiar with everything we could see, was a frequent adventure.

My dad and my brothers enjoyed jumping into the sea from the rocks at the tip of the breakwater. From there, the water looked darker due to the depth. I think the depth there was about 6 to 8 meters.

They jumped, then came out of the sea and repeated that feat over and over again. They really enjoyed doing so, and they looked very happy. I believe that the sensation of the jump, and maybe something seen under the water, was special to them.

My mother knew how to swim, but she never left the shore. Not feeling the sand at the bottom on her feet, caused her certain fear or perhaps anxiety. She was my excuse for not going with the others to jump off the breakwater. I preferred to stay close to mom, and play with her, because she enjoyed the sea in a contagious way.

Perhaps my nerves about jumping from the breakwater were based on the fear of tripping on top of an underwater rock and breaking some bone. One of my sisters had already had an accident, jumping from there, falling on top of a rock, and fracturing her little toe.

One day I decided to finally jump off the rocks of the breakwater. With my dad already in the water, I gained courage and jumped. What an incredible feeling I had when I entered the sea, which had invited me for so long!

I think that was the magical moment that made me recognize that there was a wonderful connection between the sea and me.

In this way, having the sea present in our daily landscape, enjoying its warm and calm waters, swimming constantly and acquiring more confidence and love for the ocean, a great part of my teens passed by.

The Big Decision

It was not until many years later, when I was already at a mature age, near my 50s, when I decided to venture and enter that wonderful world of the BLUE (as some of us, divers, call it), It was then when I began to know a little more of the submarine world.

Since then, I began to enjoy an incredible experience, not only because of the beauty that the marine flora and fauna offers to us, but also because I discovered a set of emotions and sensations that were totally new to me, that I had never experienced before.

To start diving safely, I had to prepare myself technically, and little by little, I became certified to be able to venture into this exciting world.

Thought different courses I learned the proper use of diving equipment (the regulator or mouthpiece, the mask, the pressure gauge, the dive computer, the compass, the BCD vest, etc.). I also learned underwater swimming techniques, safety techniques in diving, and these allowed me, in turn, to gain confidence in my trips under the sea.

I remember that diving into the sea for the first time with diving equipment was not an easy task. I wondered if I would know how to breathe well with those devices, I also wondered if I would know how to clean the mask, if it fogged up or if water got into it. ¿Could I compensate for the pressure in my ears during the descent?

Despite my training, all these doubts would come to my mind, which was natural, because it was something new for me.

However, knowing that there would always be an instructor nearby, with the necessary knowledge to help me if ever an unforeseeable situation arose, gave me great peace of mind.

Little by little I began to experience getting closer to the fish, adopting, with discipline, the appropriate behavior of not touching the corals or the marine fauna and flora.

Among us divers, we always say that "at the bottom of the sea you only take photos and only leave bubbles."

I became aware of the importance of respecting my surroundings and this wonderful environment and I learned to enjoy it by swimming relaxed, advancing only with the impulse of the gentle action of my legs.

I also began to experience that feeling of relaxation, to observe the calm, to appreciate the silence and stillness of the blue world. I started to feel good, comfortable almost like a fish in water, with that great sensation that you are part of marine life.

I also began to overcome those initial fears and that allowed me to feel proud of myself.

The fascinating feeling of floating in the sea, without perceiving the action of gravity, and the privilege of being able to have so many great experiences at the bottom of the sea, are, for me, a gift from God and Mother Nature.

These beginnings of my diving experience, marked in me, a great desire to explore deeper the underwater world.

Recounting my experiences about each dive into the ocean and the wonder of the trip to the deep sea, revives in me a wealth of emotions as if I were once again immersed into the Blue.

Although diving is an extreme sport, if we do it with the appropriate equipment and always following the safety instructions during diving, scuba diving can become a safe, very attractive and satisfying hobby.

It is considered a high-risk extreme sport, since when diving into the sea we must always consider that there are several risks, but we minimize these risks through knowledge and good practice.

How does diving affect our body?

When descending into the sea, the pressure of the water increases over our entire body. Excessive pressure can cause serious problems in our organs. especially in our lungs.

A simple way to understand pressure is to know that, at the surface, at sea level, our body experiences 1 atmospheric pressure, but as we descend, this pressure increases approximately 1 atmosphere for every 10 meters. That is, at 10 meters deep we have a pressure of 2 atmospheres on our body, 3 at 20 meters, 4 at 30 meters and so on.

When one begins to descend into the sea, given this pressure, the lungs begin to shrink and compress.

During a dive, the pressure then increases as we descend, and this affects the air we have in our lungs.

Oxygen, which is lighter, is affected by compression and decreases, while carbon dioxide, which is denser, expands and can become more difficult to discard. This can cause a decrease in the amount of oxygen available to our body, which in turn can affect the performance and safety of the dive.

Apart from these gases, I must also mention nitrogen. Nitrogen is a gas that is normally present in the air we breathe, it is absorbed by the lungs and goes to the circulatory system, where it is used to supply oxygen to the body's tissues.

When we descend into the sea, nitrogen also plays a crucial role during deep dives.

As we gain depth, the pressure increases, and nitrogen concentrates and can accumulate in the form of bubbles in the body tissue and arteries. This process is known as "barotraumatic diving" and can cause serious problems such as "decompression sickness" or "deep sea sickness." However, there are techniques to avoid getting sick, which permit us to eliminate those bubbles, just before reaching the sea surface.

This technique is called decompression or safety stops, which I will explain later.

Another risk of scuba diving, when you do not yet have experience, is learning how to breathe through your mouth with the help of diving equipment. Many people find it difficult to breathe only through their mouth, and therefore, it is necessary to learn how to use the regulator.

When we are underwater, we do not have access to air like we do when we are on the surface. Therefore, one depends on scuba diving equipment to obtain air and oxygen.

If something goes wrong with the equipment, or if it is not used properly, there could be dangerous consequences.

Breathing through the mouth through the regulator is often a challenge that we must overcome.

Learning to Scuba Dive

To descend into the sea, you must learn to scuba dive. First, I had to take a course that not only allowed me to know the details of scuba diving, but also gave me very valuable information about diving techniques, the proper use of equipment, safety techniques and helped me develop several skills to dive safely and satisfactorily.

Therefore, any inexperienced person must take a simple course to be able to do scuba diving. This usually consists of watching a video and complementing it with a talk from an experienced and certified instructor. Afterwards, a practice will be carried out.

To obtain adequate training in scuba diving, there is a wide variety of courses, from the simplest to the most specialized, and they are taught by certified instructors.

These courses are generally offered by recognized international associations or organizations such as PADI, SSI, CMAS, NAUI, IDA, to name a few.

With these organizations you not only learn how to scuba dive, but you can also get certified. By becoming certified, a person acquires the skills and knowledge to dive at an international level, and according to the level of certification acquired, they will be able to enjoy everything from simple dives to deeper, more complex ones, and even become a professional.

In my case, I have several certifications, but they are all for recreational diving.

The initial experience to learn the basics of scuba diving is through a Discovery course. This is not a certification, but it is essential to rent equipment and dive into the sea.

The Discovery lessons allow you to explore up to a depth of 10-12 meters, and it can be credited as your first open water dive towards your initial diving certification.

After this program you may opt to get certifications through a few recreational diving courses like Open Water Diver OWD, Advanced Open Water Diver AOWD, Master Scuba Diver MSD, Rescue Diver RD, Enriched air Diver ED NITROX, etc.

These names are mainly those used by PADI, since each organization or association of those already mentioned uses its own names or denomination, but the principle of learning and certification is quite similar.

There are also short courses for cave diving, night diving, digital photography, navigating with a compass, exploring shipwrecks, deep diving, etc.

Additionally, there are other more specialized courses such as professional diving, technical diving, research, and exploration diving, etc. But in this book, I will limit myself to recounting my dives and experiences, which are only related to recreational diving.

Discovery is a short course that can last 2 to 3 hours. With it you will learn the proper use of each piece of diving equipment, its functions and how to use it properly. Likewise, you learn about mouth-breathing techniques, and how to enjoy and relax while swimming underwater.

In addition, emphasis is placed on the fundamental importance of always breathing normally, through the equipment, without pauses or haste, and the importance of always doing the dives accompanied by another person.

As part of the initial Discovery course, after the theory, a short practice is carried out in confined waters, that can be a swimming pool or even on the shore of the beach, where the waters are calm and clear.

There, breathing through the mouth will be practiced under the water, with the help of your regulator.

Likewise, there is a practical review of how to recover the mask, in case you lose it for some reason, how to clean it if it fogs up, or gets water in it; how to reach the main regulator if it comes off, how to fill the diving vest or BCD with air and how to empty it so we can sink towards the seabed.

Also in this course you learn how to compensate, which is the way to make the ears adapt to the pressure of the water, as we sink. This is a fundamental step to be able to go down, and it is achieved with practice and patience.

The instructor will ensure that each diver acquires this knowledge and masters the most basic practices.

At the end of this practice in safe or confined waters, the next step is to do the immersion in open waters.

There we put into practice the knowledge received, as well as the initiation of jumping into the sea. There are several ways to jump into the sea from the boat.

This open water diving is done accompanied by one or several instructors, depending on the size of the group of divers starting out in scuba diving.

The instructors will check that everyone has their equipment ready, that the air passage from the tank bottle to the regulator is open, that the BCD has enough air to allow you to float when jumping into the water, and they will be accompanying you on the descent and during the process of adaptation of the ears to the pressure, or compensation.

Buoyancy is also practiced in this dive since it is important to stay floating underwater without reaching the bottom. Buoyancy is achieved by balancing the volume of air we have in the vest or BCD with the extra weight called ballast, which we use to descend.

The Discovery course can be done as many times as you want, but if you want to achieve more knowledge and go deeper, you will need to be certified as a diver.

Beginning my Scuba Diving Adventure

My first underwater experience was through a Discovery course which I took in an archipelago or group of islands, located off the coast of Venezuela, called Los Roques.

The extraordinary crystalline and blue waters, of various shades of blue, were really what led me to make the decision to satisfy that lifelong curiosity, to undertake my adventure in recreational scuba diving, and finally be prepared to go down to the depths and enjoy the wonders that you can encounter at the bottom of the sea.

At Los Roques there are a variety of islets where scuba diving is constantly practiced.

Given the tropical climate in this region, any time of the year is perfect to visit its beaches and to go scuba diving. The sea temperature is always warm and can vary between 25°C and 30°C. Its waters are generally calm and so crystal clear that underwater visibility can reach up to about 30 meters. This was then the ideal place to spend a few days near the beach.

My sister and I had planned a trip to this Venezuelan archipelago, to get to know it and enjoy its beaches. We both left Caracas with our children. She took her 2 children, and I went with my two teenage daughters too.

We flew for less than an hour and arrived at Gran Roque, which is the only habitable island in the entire archipelago, mainly fishermen live there. The population of Los Roques does not exceed 1,200 people, but it hosts tourists throughout the entire year.

We stayed in a beautiful inn, one of the many in town. There they offered us various trips to the beaches and nearby keys. Among their proposals was the possibility of taking a basic course of scuba diving. Of course, our children jumped with excitement, and so did I, knowing that we had in front of us the opportunity to dive.

We all agreed, and we immediately took the Discovery lessons. The class began with a video and a talk, and as I explained previously, we did our practice in calm waters on the seashore and later we went to the open sea.

! That's when the adventure really began!!

We started our first dive in Boca de Cote, a key located a little far from Gran Roque, but truly a spectacular place.

Upon arrival, we first got ready with our diving suits, we proceeded to check that the equipment was ready, that the air passage from the tank was open for breathing, and that we had enough air in the vest or BCD to be able to float when jumping into the sea.

Then, jumping to the sea was quite a learning experience, for me it was easier to do it sitting on the edge of the boat and letting myself fall backwards into the water.

Already floating in the sea, we held on to the rope tied to the boat that reached the bottom, with the anchor.

To begin the descent, I took the BCD trachea located on the left side of my chest and began to let some air out of the vest, I immediately began to descend.

While holding on to the rope, the next thing was to begin to compensate and help my ears handle the pressure. This is achieved by pinching your nose with both fingers, above the mask, and swallowing saliva several times. I went down a little and my ears started ringing.

The instructor let me know through signs that I needed to climb up about 30 centimeters, hold the rope, and resume the technique of swallowing saliva.

As you swallow saliva, the pressure in your ears equals the pressure in the water. I did this exercise repeatedly, going down and up a little, when necessary, until I got my ears feeling totally fine.

Compensating took me a while, but I was able to achieve it with practice. The interesting thing about all this is that as you dive often, your body learns and memorizes how to compensate in such a way, that every time you do a dive, compensating becomes easier and you can achieve it almost automatically.

As we tried to get down to the bottom, my sister could not compensate, even though she tried many times. Between the ringing in her ears and the waves of the sea, which were not so strong, she gave up and decided "that this sport was not for her." It was necessary for her to return to the boat. Despite my insisting that she tried again, my sister got into the boat.

I continued with my descent and to my surprise, when I finally reached the seabed, everyone: my daughters and my nephew and niece were already down there waiting for me. Really, young people have more learning capacity than people my age, I thought.

At the bottom of the sea, at about a depth of 9 meters, we all got together and waited for the signs of the instructors.

Immediately, I started to feel weird, I was having a panic attack. I was very nervous and afraid that I wouldn't be able to go on. Horrible thoughts invaded my mind about situations that could happen to us down there, at the bottom of the sea, and I thought that I did not have the experience to overcome them.

I was really scared. My body was starting to feel cold, and my mind was flying with terror thoughts. I signaled to the instructor, and he saw the terror in my eyes, and then he made some signs instructing me to calm down.

I then began to do a mental exercise, I told myself: "I'm fine, I'm breathing perfectly, I'm with experienced instructors, I feel physically well, I must calm down and continue forward with this, which I have dreamed of for such a long time."

I stayed like this for a few minutes, making an effort to put myself together, until I began to calm down and regained confidence hoping that everything would be fine. After a while, I signaled the instructor that I was feeling better and that we could continue. I think the fact that my sister had given up earlier, affected me in some way.

When the instructor made sure that I was already over that moment, he showed us where to go and started correcting our posture when swimming. The proper posture is to swim horizontally, without using your arms or hands to propel yourself.

As you swim, you boost yourself only by moving your stretched legs gently like scissors. The arms must remain close to our body during the swim, unless you take photos or must make a sign.

While being underwater the way to communicate is through internationally established manual signs, with your hands and arms, and it is necessary to know them. For example, there are signs to indicate the following:

Let's Descend

Are you OK?

I'm fine.

I can't compensate.

I don't feel well.

Stop there!

Check that out!

Come to me

Let's go there.

Stay together.

How much air do you have left?

I have little air.

I have half a bottle.

Let's go up.

WE ALSO LEARNED HOW to achieve neutral buoyancy. That is, floating without sinking or ascending involuntarily, that is, always floating at the same desired level and only rising or diving at will.

After this hands-on learning, the underwater tour was like entering an immense and amazing museum.

We stayed at a depth of about 8-9 meters and began to see the marine plants, with their green, yellow, and brown colors. We also observed small fish that snaked through the plants. We saw black sea urchins, cylindrical sponges, and as we moved forward, we came to a beautiful coral reef with beautiful patches of orange, green, and yellow colors that, because of their tiny movements, looked as if they were breathing.

The day was sunny, and the sun's rays penetrated the sea, illuminating the entire seabed, making the colors seem brighter.

We stopped to contemplate so much beauty, take photos, play underwater enjoying the lack of gravity in our bodies, and we began to observe small fish that came and went and pecked at the corals in the reef.

We saw schools of cobbler and shad passing by that crossed our path and did not even flinch from our presence. Likewise, we saw a solitary barracuda and several parrotfish with their striking green and orange colors feeding from the corals.

I was already feeling quite comfortable under the sea. Without a doubt, it was a first experience full of intense emotions, many impressions, and a lot of learning.

In my various subsequent dives, I never again felt that unpleasant feeling of panic and fear.

I had lived a horrible and difficult experience, but I learned that, thanks to self-control, which I carried out in time and with the support of the instructor, I was able to overcome it and continue forward. I don't think I will ever forget that episode.

Furthermore, the practice of self-control has helped me overcome other unexpected situations that occurred to me on other dives, which I will relate later.

When we surfaced, after about 40 minutes of this swim, our boat was waiting for us very close by. We inflated our BCDs to float and swam to get there. Upon arrival we found fresh water to hydrate ourselves. We rested on our way to Gran Roque, where we would have some lunch.

During the return and lunch, we discussed our experiences with joy and enthusiasm.

Each one of us had something to talk about this fabulous encounter under the sea. What some of us did not see, others saw. There was so much to see and at the same time, to be careful to do things right, that we couldn't get to see everything around us.

I told about my panic attack underwater, which not everyone had noticed.

The instructor then showed us photos of the fish we had seen, so we began to become familiar with their names.

In the afternoon, we were quite tired. The immersion and stress of learning and practicing so much exhausted us, therefore, we preferred to go to the beach and relax a little.

The next day, my nephew, my niece and my youngest daughter and me were ready to continue our adventure. My eldest daughter decided to stay with my sister and enjoy a walk on the island, and climb to Cerro del Faro, from where you can see the immensity and beauty of this archipelago, which is classified as a national park.

During the next two days we continued our scuba diving, enjoying other dives in keys near Gran Roque, such as Francisquí, El Morrito and Rabusquí.

In Francisquí we did another dive in a natural pool located there. Very soon we arrived at a bronze statue of a Virgin called the Virgin of the Valley, who is the protective saint of that region, particularly, of the Venezuelan Caribbean Sea.

This statue is located about 4 meters deep in very clear blue waters. Given the shallow depth the sunlight penetrated and reflected its rays in a magical way under the sea, making shapes on the white sand. We were able to swim and enjoy that beautiful statue for a while, which by the shape of her arms, seemed to be blessing the ocean.

After resting and hydrating on the surface, we proceeded to make our next dive. We did this one at El Morrito, which is like a sunken mountain, very close to the main island Gran Roque.

As we jumped into the sea from the boat, we saw a sunken sailboat and we approached it to observe it. We did not enter it, but it was very interesting to see how various corals have been forming and have populated its surface.

The fauna on this key is simply spectacular. We saw a great variety of fish such as parrotfish, biting parts of the corals, and schools of pomfrets swimming together in coordination.

Very close to the coral reef there were snappers, and very small fish of different colors. Also, we were delighted to see a beautiful hawksbill turtle that, upon seeing us, swam out and rose to the surface.

Here in El Morrito, among the rocks I saw a lionfish for the first time. This fish is strikingly beautiful due to its large crest of brown, red and white stripes. While we watched it and took photos, it remained motionless, as if it was there to be photographed. This is a fish that has invaded our Caribbean seas, since its natural habitat is the South Pacific and the Indian Ocean.

It is so harmful to our ecosystem, that I have dedicated a complete chapter later in this book, about the threat posed by the presence of this fish in our oceans and seas.

El Morrito is famous for housing crustaceans and lobsters. These tend to hide under rocks, and despite our efforts, we only managed to see a pair of antennae of a lobster hidden under some large stones, but at this time, we could not see it completely.

On this dive, for some reason water got into my mask and it needed to be cleared. The technique of clearing the mask while underwater is very simple and it is not necessary to remove it from the face. Just by pressing hard on the top of it, against your forehead, and looking up, you blow hard through your nose and all the water comes out! This exercise is easy and very useful.

El Morrito offers a great variety of flora and fauna. We spent a lot of time admiring the underwater landscape and its flora, and still looking for crustaceans.

Almost at the end of this walk, our instructor spotted the antennae of a lobster hidden in the rocks, and he decided to make it come out. First, he punched one side of the rock with a stick, and with his other hand he placed a hand net in front of the lobster. She then got out and ended up trapped in the mesh.

He showed us the crustacean, which was fairly small. We took pictures and videos and after a few seconds, he freed it and let it go.

After about 40 minutes enjoying underwater, we were about to use up all the air in our aluminum tanks, so our instructor decided it was time to surface.

Already resting in our boat, the instructor explained to us that even though it is allowed to hunt lobsters in this area, the one he had caught was very small, and by rule, it is prohibited to hunt them until they reach at least 20 cm. long.

I think we were all happy with the release of this, our very first lobster seen under the sea.

Our last dive in this paradisiacal archipelago was in Cayo Rabusquí. The clear, turquoise waters there allowed us to observe the beauty of its fauna from the distance.

In Rabusquí we were happily surprised to see at the bottom of the sand, at a very shallow depth, an impressive variety of starfish. They could be seen even with a snorkel, and each one of them were different, with their proper colors and marks and shapes.

The man who was transporting us on the boat, told us later that among the fishermen of the area there is a belief: they assure that whoever finds a 6-pointed starfish, on their first trip to Rabusquí, must make a wish, because it is a! sign of good luck! I particularly saw nothing but 5-pointed starfish.

My Special Diving Place

After the great initial experience in Los Roques, many of my dives were mainly in Chichiriviche de la Costa, which is a beautiful beach in a small bay for fishermen and divers.

Chichi, as we affectionately call it, is in the coastal state of La Guaira, in northern Venezuela.

Chichiriviche is only about a 35 minutes' drive to the coast from Caracas, where I lived. The sea waters are calm and mostly warm between 23°C and 28°C all year round, and it is a regular meeting point for many scuba divers, so I adopted this place as my favorite and convenient place to go diving quite frequently.

I made countless scuba dives on these beaches and began to meet other divers. I even became friends and a member of a club of divers related to the company where I used to work.

With these fellow divers I perfected the knowledge and skills of this sport and together we planned to go down to the beach from Caracas several times a month. The practice of scuba diving was already becoming a wonderful hobby.

Even during this time, I only had the initial Discovery diving course and not any scuba certification yet.

Meeting other people, who equally loved the sport, and hearing from them their exciting stories under the sea in Chichiriviche, I thought that, if I got certified, I could dive deeper and also enjoy other scenarios.

My fellow divers always talked about the sunken pieces on that beach and nearby, which are there, not only for the enjoyment of the divers, but also to boost coral formations and therefore attract great variety of fish.

Since I did not have the certification to go down to the depths where these sunken pieces were, I decided that it was time for me to continue learning and to become an Open Water Diver certified.

I didn't do it immediately, but a few months later while I was enjoying a cruise in the Caribbean, which had started in Miami, Florida and planned to visit the islands of Puerto Rico, Saint Thomas, Bahamas, and Labadíe in Haiti.

On the boat of this cruise, I discovered that they had a small diving center and they taught PADI classes and issued certifications. So, I decided to take the Open Water Diver OWD course. I thought it was the perfect time to do it.

I did the theoretical part and with the instructor, I did the dives on the island of Saint Thomas.

The waters of this beautiful island are of a light turquoise tone, very calm and I remember them having a very pleasant temperature. Its crystal-clear waters allowed us to see far away.

I had the opportunity to descend to about 14 meters, where there was a sunken fishing boat and a sailboat available for divers to visit, which we did.

After a short swim, we stopped to perform several underwater safety exercises, such as passing through some hoops of different diameters, to familiarize ourselves with the dimension of our equipment.

This exercise allows the scuba diver to calculate the size of the equipment they are carrying, not to get trapped or trip when entering or exiting a shipwreck, or a narrow area during their underwater trip.

The idea is to go through these hoops without stumbling. Pushing yourself only with the movement of your legs and feet. Another exercise consisted of kneeling on the seabed and removing the mask and putting it back on while being underwater.

We also practiced removing the regulator from the mouth, recovering it, and putting it back into the mouth, without swallowing water, to be prepared in case of any unexpected situation ever happened under the sea.

At the end of these practices, we dedicated ourselves to observing the fauna that lives and moves inside both boats. The fish would come out and flutter around to return to the same place, where perhaps they felt safer.

Very close to the seabed, next to some branches, I had an encounter with my first seahorse. The seahorse is a really beautiful creature. It is much smaller than I always imagined.

This one barely measured about 12 cm, it was brown in color, and it remained standing there anchored with its tail to one of the branches of the plant, and it remained like that calmly, without moving and without being disturbed by my presence.

I also noticed a beautiful green turtle swimming gently, very close to me, which, upon seeing me, changed course.

If there are coral reefs in Saint Thomas, I did not have the opportunity to see them, but we did see many marine plants and I was able to observe a sea cucumber up close that was crawling on the bottom. We also saw schools of yellow fish and blue/yellow fish that inadvertently passed by us.

By the end of these dives in Saint Thomas, I had already met the requirements to be OWD certified.

Now being certified as an Open Water Diver, I did several dives, quite frequently in Chichiriviche de la Costa, because it was the best-known site for me, and as I said before, relatively close to home.

Subsequently, I was able to descend to other depths not previously reached and finally, was able to go down to see and enjoy the many statues and sunken pieces that I had heard most of my friends talk about but was not able to see since I did not have the appropriate certification.

At this beach, given that it is very popular among divers, there are several pieces made of bronze, cement, or other material, submerged between 16 and 22 meters deep, that other divers have placed, for the enjoyment of those who practice this sport, and to promote the growth of coral reefs.

The most notable ones that I visited repeatedly, after obtaining my PADI OWD certification, are:

The Cristo de La Costa, (The Christ of the Coast) located at a depth of 22 meters. This statue, with its arms extended as if inviting a hug, is quite colonized with corals and it is also almost completely covered with rosaries and necklaces that many divers have left there. This beautiful statue is located standing at the so-called Chichiriviche wall, in one of its corners. This is truly a spectacular site to visit.

About 14 meters deep, is the Neptune Flute, which is a tribute that a group of divers located in 2003, to honor their diving instructor Carlos Dinar. It is located on a low pedestal, where you can also see a plaque of gratitude. This is a must-see for anyone doing its Open Water Diver course.

Continuing towards 16 meters deep, we find the new statue of the Virgin of the Valley, which due to its short time there, still does not house many corals. However, there is a belief that if you visit it, everything will turn out well for you that day.

At around 19 meters deep, the Eiffel Tower is located on a sort of flat area, almost in solitary. This tower measures just under 2 meters high. Nearby there is very little marine flora. However, a visit to this tower provides the opportunity to see abundant and beautiful marine fauna. Starfish by the dozens are often seen on the seabed there and I have even seen squid swimming in groups.

Getting close and visiting these statues and their surroundings truly provides an extraordinary experience.

In the waters of Chichiriviche Bay the marine fauna is impressive, and very rich in variety. Constantly, one comes across flute fish, puffer fish, sea cucumbers, countless small fish of different colors, coral snakes, and some schools of squid. Parrot fish are seen very frequently, showing off their green and red colors. This species is essential for keeping coral reefs healthy, and in Chichiriviche they are abundant throughout the year.

Very close to the wall where the Cristo de La Costa is located, we had an encounter with a magnificent octopus, which appeared one day when we stopped by to observe corals. It noticed our presence, came out of its hiding and we could see its light pink and beige colors, but it didn't stop, and immediately it got away from us without feeling threatened.

During the first months of the year, I remember that at a depth of about 4 to 6 meters there are often dozens of starfish very close to the seashore. It is impressive to see so many and all different from each other; They gather in that place because they receive the sun's rays almost directly and enjoy the temperature of the water at this time of year.

People with snorkels and even divers often come to see these enigmatic beings.

Unfortunately, lionfish are already established in this beach.

Although sport fishing is extremely restricted in Venezuela, the only one that is practiced legally and without permits is the capturing of lionfish. Lionfish is a species that has invaded our seas in America, and therefore it is very common to see divers catching them with spears.

In conclusion, Chichiriviche is a perfect place to practice diving all year round. It is very close to the city, and it is located in a beautiful bay.

My group of friends and colleagues considered it our favorite place, for any weekend. The people of the town are very nice, there is an excellent fellowship among divers, and we always felt like "fish in water" when we were submerged. We knew its waters and sea life quite well and visited them repeatedly. However, there was constantly something new to see around there.

On these beaches there are times when the whale shark is sighted, which despite its large size, is quite harmless. Unfortunately, so far, I haven't been lucky enough to see any.

The Lionfish

I decided to spend some time writing this chapter about lionfish, because, from the point of view of the marine ecosystem on our Caribbean seas, this fish is becoming a great threat.

Lionfish is not a native species of the Caribbean Sea where I have seen it, but a terrible invader.

This fish is native to the South Pacific and the Indian Ocean. However, they were seen for the first time off the coast of Florida in 1985.

Starting in 2009, they began to be seen on the coasts of the Southern Caribbean and even in the Gulf of Mexico, and their presence in the Mediterranean Sea and much of the coast of Brazil has already been reported.

It is estimated that lionfish reached the coasts of Florida after Hurricane Andrew, which swept captive specimens into the sea in aquariums and boats that contained them.

Lionfish is a very exotic fish, of great and striking beauty for its large antennae and fins with white, red and brown lines. It has a large crest of poisonous spines that it uses to defend itself from predators. By the way, a sting from one of these spines can cause sores, a lot of pain and swelling for several days.

Lionfish are a dreadful predator that feeds on parrotfish, snapper, dorado, grouper and mollusks, crabs, and other invertebrates. It also devours coral reefs and the smallest fish that serve as food for other fish, since they eat voraciously and excessively.

It is, therefore, an invasive fish that endangers the species found in the Atlantic Ocean and in the Caribbean Sea.

For this reason, lionfish are considered a dangerous predator. It has already altered the food chains of the seas it invades, destroying native species.

One problem is that there are no known major predators in this region, to lionfish, outside of its natural habitat, and that is already affecting and threatening our underwater diversity.

Some experts consider that this fish is one of the most harmful marine species for the ecosystems it has invaded.

Unfortunately, they reproduce at an alarming rate, releasing thousands of eggs a year, so their species has been spreading rapidly.

I have seen lionfish on several of my dives in Chuchiriviche de La Costa, in Los Roques and in the waters of Florida. When it swims it does it very gently and very close to the seabed, as if it is searching for its prey.

Lionfish are mostly solitary and almost always are perched on some coral, on sea rocks and even inside shipwrecks. Due to its location, it is not a fish that can be caught with a hook.

The only "predator" it has outside its natural habitat, therefore, is mankind, and the need to selectively hunt them is becoming an urgent priority.

To combat lionfish, various organizations and conservation groups have been created, which consider that selective hunting of these invasive species is the only effective way to reduce their expansion.

Some recreational divers today take to spearing them in an effort to keep the lionfish population under control. However, the natural venom of this fish requires divers to be well trained and use safe ways to catch and transport it.

Now knowing more about this invasive fish, I had the opportunity, on several of my dives, both in Chichiriviche de la Costa and other Venezuelan beaches, to accompany groups of divers, armed with their spears to hunt and kill lionfish.

In one of my dives in Venezuela, at about a depth of 16 meters towards the bottom of the seabed, between the coral reef we found one lionfish perched, almost hidden between rocks and the corals.

Beyond, hidden on the side of a small shipwreck, was another larger one. We didn't have to swim far to find another one that was quietly floating near some rocks.

Catching these fish was not difficult. Once you see them, they remain calm, as if ignoring their surroundings. These fish are not caught with a hook, or while they are swimming.

To trap them it is necessary to have a good pole spear and when you see them calm and still, it is the time to spike the spear with some force into the animal's body. After being speared the lionfish is put into a puncture-resistant container device to prevent getting hurt.

It was hard for me to accept that we must fight and kill these animals. But the sad reality of finding and catching three lionfish, in less than 40 minutes diving, made me realize that unfortunately, they have already been spreading rapidly.

The practice of pursuing them with a spear has been increasing more and more, and it is allowed to do so in most Caribbean countries, given the importance of combating this evil, which tends to devour any marine life it encounters.

Therefore, it is quite common to see divers go to the bottom of the sea with spears and equipment, to bring them to the surface, without running the risk of being pricked by the fish's poisonous spines.

In the state of Florida there is a festival every year, in which the main activity is diving and hunting these invaders. There are even competitions among divers to see which group manages to hunt the most lionfish.

At these events, educational speeches are also given to spread the importance of combating this species in our American seas, and to raise awareness about the need to keep our marine ecosystem healthy.

Another way to control lionfish numbers is to consume them. Its meat is very white, and its flavor is quite pleasant. It is rapidly becoming a favorite dish in some coastal areas, since several restaurants cook them, and it already appears on their menu.

Unfortunately, hunting these fish one by one or consuming them will not help reduce the numbers drastically. But efforts are being made while experts find a better solution to eradicate or reduce the proliferation of lionfish in our seas, out of its natural habitat, before it is too late.

Cleaning The Seabed

Not all diving is for fun, enjoying the marine life and the underwater wonders. There are a variety of activities that can take us to the bottom of the seas, in an effort to contribute to keep our marine environment clean and safe.

I had the great opportunity to participate in a program related to the conservation of beaches and the marine ecosystem.

In September of 2014, my fellow divers and I were invited by a foundation related to Buceo in Venezuela, to participate in their Clean Waves Program, which they carry out annually.

This program consists of cleaning the beaches and the seabed, and it is generally organized for the month of September to celebrate the World's Beaches Day. On this occasion the event was held in Macuto, La Guaira State, in Venezuela.

More than 50 scuba divers participated voluntarily in this significant program, cleaning several beaches.

In Particular, my group of fellow divers and I were assigned to do the underwater tracking and cleaning of Camurichico Beach, in Macuto.

While a group of marine ecologists gave awareness talks about the ecology of our beaches and seas, a group of volunteers swept the sands, collected, and discarded trash and we, the scuba divers, submerged into the sea to collect inorganic trash from the seabed.

We were handed large nylon mesh type bags to collect the inorganic waste that was accumulated at the bottom of the sea and contaminating our beaches.

We entered the sea walking from the shore, with our nylon mesh bags, to start our activity.

We had dived in and began to fill our bags with all that waste that was accumulated mainly at depths between 2 and 8 meters. The amount of trash under de sea was impressive.

We collected, among others, countless aluminum cans, paper, rags, plastic and glass bottles of soft drinks, beer and water, and even there were diapers, etc.

As we filled up our mesh bags we surfaced, to the shore and there was a group of volunteers who received our full bags from us, and would give us another empty one, to return and continue with the activity.

The event took place in a very pleasant and enjoyable way, there was music at the beach and many people were swimming nearby. Every time a diver came out to the surface to deliver the full bag and receive an empty one, the bathers applauded, cheering us. It was funny and to me it seemed very typical of our Venezuelan idiosyncrasy.

I continued doing my dives for about an hour, until I consumed all the air in my tank.

As a whole, at those beaches alone, little more than 500 kgs. of inorganic waste were collected, being mainly aluminum cans.

The organizers of this event were very satisfied with the results of the Clean Waves program, and we, the divers, were more than happy to be able to participate in such an important activity.

Diving into the Depths

Continuing with my training as a scuba diver and enjoying different marine scenarios at the same time, I decided to take the Advanced Open Water Diver AOWD course.

The AOWD certification opened the doors for me to do deeper dives and thus be able to see more interesting places. With my diving friends from Chichiriviche, I started my theoretical course and immediately did the practical part.

This new training allowed me to progress in diving techniques and learn other aspects of diving, especially at greater depths.

Among the requirements for this certification, you have to complete a deep dive, a navigation practice, buoyancy practice dive, and you can choose 3 other dives of any specialty.

In my case, I did deep diving, navigation practices, buoyancy practices and I also completed cave diving and night diving.

For these practices we went to the beaches at the Mochima National Park, located in the State of Anzoátegui, towards the northeast coast of Venezuela.

We begin on the beach with buoyancy practices, which, as I indicated previously, allows the diver to remain at the desired level, without sinking or ascending involuntarily. This is achieved by finding the appropriate balance between the ballast used and the air in your BCD. This ballast is usually a belt with some lead bars attached.

In order to determine if you have the right weight, in your ballast, you should try floating with the water at eye level. Once you exhale, you should sink a little, so that the water is just above the crown of your head.

If you sink while holding your breath, you are overweight, and you will need to adjust your ballast.

Navigation practices help you stay on track and make sure you don't get lost. Navigation can be done by following a line, using a compass, or relying on references or natural markers, both on the surface and underwater, which allow you to orient yourself, for safe and efficient exploration.

When submerged, especially in a cave or shipwreck, it is very easy to become disoriented. With instruments and good navigation practice, one can stay oriented.

For my deep dive we went out to sea where we would be able to reach a depth near 30 meters.

This dive seeks, among other things, to identify if at this depth the diver shows any sign of nitrogen narcosis, or if the diver shows some disorientation.

It is a very important test, which allows you to start recognizing your personal limits.

Likewise, it is necessary to practice all safety and control measures, such as safety or decompression stops, and buoyancy at depth.

There were two candidates for this AOWD certification, and I was one of them. Upon arriving at the site, with our instructor, we checked all our equipment, and soon he told us to jump into the sea. I, as usual, was the first one jumping backwards from the boat.

The water was not very clear, and the visibility was affected by the excess of plankton, which gave the water a greenish tone. The waters of eastern Venezuela are the coldest of all our coasts, and that morning my watch indicated that the temperature of the water was 19°C.

We descended little by little, moving our arms and legs to warm up, and soon we reached the bottom.

When we got to the bottom we sat on top of a rock and our instructor took out of his pocket a small plastic writing board and a graphite pencil. He wrote two simple mathematical operations on it and gave it to the young candidate to solve:

3+8=

5x3=

The young diver answered them, by writing the right answers on the note board, without any problem.

Immediately, the instructor proceeded to erase those operations and wrote two new ones for me, and handed me the board and pencil:

3+4=

2x5=

As soon as I placed the pencil on the board, the graphite tip broke, preventing me from writing anything. Then, given the circumstance, the instructor looked at me in the eye and gave us the signal to go up to the surface.

I refused to go up and let him know it with signs.

I knew that I could solve these operations without the pencil. I pointed out to him the first addition operation on the board and with the help of my hands and fingers I showed him the correct answer. Next, I pointed out the multiplication and gave him the answer with signs as well.

After that, we began to go up and made the first safety stop at about 15 meters from the surface. There we stopped for 2.5 minutes breathing normally. After those minutes we continued ascending 10 more meters, where we made the second stop for 3 minutes. At this point we were at about 5 meters below the water surface. Finally, after both safety stops, we got to the water surface.

These stops are very important to do and often seem to last forever. Being there floating in the middle of the water, breathing without doing anything else, for a few minutes, may seem like a waste of time, but these stops are essential for the proper functioning of our body.

Practicing safety stops gives our body the necessary time to eliminate the nitrogen bubbles that have been accumulating inside us, during deep dives. If these bubbles are not removed, they lodge in our tissues and arteries, and can cause decompression sickness, which is a debilitating and/or life-threatening condition.

These safety stops are made according to the depth reached during the dive. For dives up to 20-25 meters deep, 1 safety stop is recommended and for dives close to 30 meters deep, 2 stops are recommended.

Already on the surface, the instructor told me that, thanks to my quick reaction to solve the situation with the blunt pencil, he had been able to verify that the depth we had reached, had not affected my reaction capacity and therefore, I had passed the deep immersion test.

This made me feel very good about myself. Had I reacted differently, we would have had to repeat the deep dive, and we no longer had enough air left in our tanks to do it the same day.

The next day we planned to do a dive entering a cave. Mochima National Park, where we were, is very famous for its diversity of underwater caves and caverns.

In order to enter these caves, each diver must carry a good flashlight and follow the instructions to stay close to each other. The instructor chose to take us to the Cathedral Cave.

We sailed towards the high seas and reached the place where we were supposed to dive. As we got there, we saw the water was jammed with floating jellyfish. It is common to find jellyfish in this area, depending on the time of the year, particularly, they grow there due to the water's temperature and the presence of a lot of plankton.

To avoid the jellyfish, which looked like floating plastic bags, we changed plans and headed towards another cave, the Lighthouse Cave.

Touching the jellyfish can cause a kind of stinging, burning sensation on the skin, which can last several hours. That is a good reason why we preferred not to take the risk.

Soon after a few minutes still on the boat, we arrived at the indicated place to go down towards the Lighthouse Cave.

We jumped into the water, and it felt really cold. My watch showed the water´s temperature was 18°C. It also had that greenish tone from the plankton.

We had dived to the bottom, to about 13 meters deep, and swam a little to warm up. The visibility was not that good. After about 10 minutes swimming we were able to see, on the seabed, a dark arch-shaped shadow.

The instructor signaled to us that this was the entrance to the cave and that we should turn on our flashlights and follow him. Another instructor stood behind, following the group.

I saw how one by one of my fellow divers entering through that dark arch, and with a little fear I ventured to follow them. I didn't know what we could find there.

Upon entering, I immediately noticed that the water temperature became warmer and more pleasant.

Any initial fear dissipated in these warm waters, and I began to feel more comfortable. Immersed in the darkness of the cavern, we began to see small fish fluttering around us, shining with the light of our flashlights.

We swam a bit into the darkness and soon began to ascend. A few meters up, we emerged in a kind of dark bell, but with breathable air. There, at the water surface, we inflated our BCDs and stayed floating, resting, and taking advantage of the nice temperature of the sea, which was 25°C. A lot warmer than outside the cave.

Stuck to the rock walls we observed several fish and several small shrimps.

The upper part of the dark cave was about 6 meters above us. Upwards, we saw a small statue of some virgin placed on top of a rock, that some diver had decided to leave during his visit. This cave is also known as the Virgin's Cave.

After a while, we prepared ourselves to leave the cave. With the help of our flashlights, we submerged again. We descended some and swam for a while towards the entrance of the cave, until at a certain distance, we saw the illuminated arch that was our exit back to the clarity of the sea.

As I saw the exit, I prepared myself mentally for the change of the water´s temperature that awaited us outside the cave.

We all swam towards the arch and emerged into the clarity and of course, into the cold waters again.

This dive left me with great impressions: combining the wonder of diving with a visit to a cave was an unforgettable experience.

Plunging into darkness and finding an area of breathable air was something totally unexpected for me.

I think that the element of surprise, having a positive attitude and trusting our guide, turned out to be an important factor in making this a pleasant experience, which would be difficult to forget.

The next dive of our training would be a night dive, and with this one I would be completing the requirements for the certification I was seeking.

We prepared all our equipment, including flashlights, maracas, or diving horns and some of us even carried a knife for any eventuality.

At night we headed to an area near some cliffs with the idea of getting into a place with rocks and corals in which it is easier to find different creatures, either sleeping or being more active.

When I jumped into the water my first impression was that it was pleasant. The water near these rocky areas was not as cold as it was at high sea. Immediately as we descended, we began to see millions of luminous dots around us, it was as if we were surrounded by fireflies, but under the sea.

This phenomenon is called bioluminescence, and it is produced by a microscopic alga in plankton, whose energy generates a chemical reaction that manifests itself as light.

This microscopic alga belongs to the group of dinoflagellates called "noctiluque". It was interesting and even fun to see that, at the slightest movement of our body and arms, more lights were generated.

Being about 8 meters deep, we began our journey with our flashlights in hand and when we reached the base of the rocks, we began to see parrot fish floating peacefully, as they were asleep.

We saw some sea snakes moving around the rocks and a couple of octopuses. Octopuses tend to be more active at night when they go hunting. We saw a calm eel, which, when illuminated by our flashlight, decided to hide out among the rocks.

Night diving changes the way we see marine life. At night, the marine world seems more beautiful, different, colorful, and mysterious.

The experience and the tranquility of night diving cannot be compared to any other form of scuba diving, and it presents you with another perspective of this fascinating world. The calm of the underwater environment at night provides a very serene and relaxing experience.

Diving at night is a completely different experience. It is a great way to see some of the creatures that are dormant during the day and become active at night.

Night diving requires additional skills, safety precautions, and greater awareness of your surroundings.

Since darkness creates additional risks, it is recommended to be always close to your fellow divers, and to stay oriented. Being close means observing your colleagues and frequently making sure that everything is fine.

During this night dive we had a stressful experience. One of our dive buddies got tangled in something at the bottom of the sea and stayed behind the group.

Upon noticing his absence, I was worried and concerned so I called the attention of the rest of us, using my diving maraca that makes noise, and immediately the others approached me.

Making signs, I let them know of the absence of one of our fellow divers, so we began to look around us. Since we did not see him nearby, we decided to go back together, with the idea of finding him. In situations like these at night, it is not advisable to separate or to split up.

We all swam for about 20 meters on our way back, when we were able to identify him. As he saw our flashlight nearby, he started to move his body and arms to generate bioluminescence, so we could see him.

It turned out that he had lost his flashlight and as he descended towards the rocks to try to find it, one of his fins and his foot had gotten tangled in some kind of fisherman's net and he couldn't get free.

Not having a knife or even a device to make noise, he was left behind. A few minutes later, he started moving his arms and body to generate bioluminescence, hoping that we could see him, since he could already see in the distance, the lights of our flashlights.

After a short swim we reached him and freed him by cutting part of that mesh and provided our help to reassure him. He had not panicked, nor had he yet decided to remove his fin from his boot to ascend, but he was quite scared, so we all decided to go up to the surface.

From this experience we learned the importance of being well equipped when diving, especially at night, and being aware of each other. Thanks to bioluminescence, we found our partner in a fairly short time.

I thanked God that this incident was nothing more than a big scare.

At the end of this series of dives I had met all the requirements and obtained my PADI Advanced Open Water Diver AOWD certification.

DIVING WITH NITROX or enriched air.

A few months later, I took a trip to Cabo San Lucas, on the west coast of Mexico, with the idea of visiting the town, the beaches, doing some scuba diving, and obtaining an additional certification for diving with enriched air, also known as Nitrox.

Enriched air is a mixture of air that contains less nitrogen and more oxygen than normal air. Normal air contains 21% Oxygen.

With Nitrox, by breathing less nitrogen, the tissues of our body absorb nitrogen to a lesser extent, and this allows us to lengthen the time we stay underwater, in shallow dives. That is, we can enjoy longer dives and shorter intervals between dives on the surface. This course or certification has become very popular because of these advantages.

For example, if you dive with a Nitrox mixture containing 36% oxygen, you will be able to dive for about 20 minutes longer, being at a depth near 30 meters, or one more hour, being 21 meters down. Nitrox then allows you to extend your dive time.

However, diving with enriched air limits the maximum depth to which we can descend. This limitation happens because oxygen at a certain depth is toxic. The maximum depth at which we can do the dive, with Nitrox, could be about 30 meters. However, this will depend on the percentage of oxygen in the gas mixture. Deeper dives require the use of special gases.

My experience with the use of Nitrox, given that I do not usually descend under 30 meters, has allowed me to lengthen my dives and above all it has given me the great advantage of feeling less tired at the end of a scuba diving day.

In Cabo San Lucas we visited several diving sites and I especially remember one in Cabo Pulmo, where I had the opportunity to see my first shark.

The waters of this region of the Sea of Cortez are generally not cold (approximately 23°C at this time of the year) but because it is located in the Pacific Ocean, at this latitude they are not as warm as the they are in the Caribbean Sea.

We planned this dive with a local diver guide. The plan was to look for and observe a whitetip shark that they had spotted the day before near the reefs. The whitetip shark is very common in the reefs of these coasts and usually stays at the bottom of clear waters.

We submerged about 18 meters down, and searched between the rocks for a while, until we found one shark hidden.

Our guide hit the rock near the animal, and the shark came out, and made a couple of short circles right there in front of us and hid again. It was quick, but it gave us enough time to take photos and videos.

This shark measured approximately 1.5 meters. long, with its head short and wide. It was very slender and had white markings on the tips of its fins. Because of these markings, it bears the common name whitetip shark.

The guide later explained to us that these sharks usually remain in a particular area of the reef for months or years, continually returning to the same refuge.

For that reason, it was relatively easy for him to find the shark that morning. He also told us that these fish live near reefs, because they feed on bony fish, cephalopods and crustaceans, and the largest sharks also usually eat squid and octopuses.

In this area of the Sea of Cortez, we were able to see fish such as big-eyed trevally, snappers, pig-fish, schools of large fish, and sea turtles.

Visiting Shipwrecks

For several centuries, countless ships have found their resting place in the depths of the seas and oceans. They hold great stories. Over the years they have become an unexpected and welcoming home for a wide variety of marine life.

Wreck diving gives you the unique opportunity to go back in time, visit and explore sunken pieces, which have a history, and therefore, you can learn part of their past. It also presents a set of challenges to divers and opens the doors to new experiences.

Wreck diving is a very specific type of dive that requires a series of special knowledge and skills to ensure that it is done, considering appropriate safety measures.

My first visit to a shipwreck, or a sunken ship, was on the island of Cuba very close to Varadero Beach.

This beach is famous for its very white sands and crystal-clear waters. The beach is really beautiful, full of palm trees and its coastline is very long. It measures near 20 kms.

FISHERMA'S BOAT IN Varadero, Cuba

Out to sea, near Varadero, we planned our first dive with the idea of finding this shipwreck. When we jumped into the ocean, we noticed the pleasant temperature of the water and soon we began the descent.

After a short swim, we found this fishing boat at about 12 meters down into the bottom. The boat was not too big. It was about 18 meters long and it was perched on the sand, in a small flat area. Due to its good condition for marine life, it was already a true reef, corals and several types of plants had already formed on its surface, making it the perfect shelter for countless species.

I was able to enter what had been the captain's control cabin. It was a small, but spacious room and we noticed that there were still some handles, already rusty and covered with tiny, brightly colored corals. I took some photos, being really careful of not to trip over anything.

When approaching or entering a shipwreck it is important to avoid touching or tripping over its structure.

The corals and plants that have formed on its surface are very sensitive and fragile and any contact with an external agent can damage them. Even a slight pressure from tripping over them can cause loss of coral tissue. We must always, therefore, avoid physical contact with corals and underwater species.

Additionally, if our skin gets scratches by any structure covered with coral formations or rust, a simple cut can become infected, since both the water and marine reefs contain an infinite number of microorganisms that, when coming into contact with open wounds, can cause infections.

With this no-touch rule in mind, wreck diving is extremely enjoyable and satisfying.

SPIEGEL GROVE IN SOUTH Florida, USA

On one occasion in the warm waters of southern Florida, off the coast of Key Largo, I had the opportunity to take an underwater tour and see the USS Spiegel Grove (LSD-32).

This was a United States Navy troop transport ship, which in 2002 the Navy decided to sink it in a planned and controlled manner, as part of a project to create artificial reefs, which would serve as a habitat for marine life and a site diving attraction. However, it initially did not settle upright as planned and became stranded on its side on the seabed.

Subsequently, several weeks after the sinking, a successful effort was made to move the ship and make it sit upright on the seabed.

The Spiegel Grove measures approximately 155 meters in length and has several levels that vary in depth underwater from 18 to 41 meters.

To get to know it well, it is necessary to make several dives, because due to its depth and large volume, it is not possible to visit it all in a single dive.

Furthermore, due to its large size and depth, diving in the Spiegel Grove requires advanced diving skills. Divers, therefore, must have appropriate certifications and take safety precautions.

Its upper deck is at about 18 meters below the surface of the water. The hull of the boat, which is a large labyrinth inside, is seated at 41 meters underwater. It is important to bear in mind that at the lowest level of this ship, the bottom´s sediment can rise and reduce visibility to almost zero, which can cause disorientation.

During my dive to this spectacular ship, we descended on a very sunny day. Already at 8 meters under the surface of the water, you could see its immense size sited at the bottom.

I went down with the expectation and wondering where to start my, to make the most of this visit.

I had with me a single air tank that I thought could be enough for a maximum of 20 minutes exploring the ship, given its depth (another 20 minutes of air would be to descend and ascend).

It is important to note that the depth at which you dive directly affects the duration of the air supply. The deeper the dive, the higher the water pressure and therefore the faster the air is consumed.

I know my air consumption rate a little and I knew that, on the descent, while I was compensating and looking down at the ship, I had already consumed some of my air. So I estimated that I could explore the Spiegel Grove for about 20 minutes, without going down to 40 meters. I also knew that later, I would need enough air to ascend and make the safety stops.

Upon reaching the deck of the Spiegel Grove we dispersed, but our guide was keeping an eye on all of us.

I decided to explore the deck a little to see the remains of equipment that were still rusty and covered with corals, vegetation and thus housing lots of small fish.

Afterwards, I began to swim towards the stern of the ship with the idea of going around the ship and exploring more areas. However, a huge green moray eel appeared to me from nowhere. It remained calm but since I was in its habitat, I decided to get away in order not to disturb it. This one was perhaps more than six feet long.

I have seen moray eels on several occasions, and if you don't bother them, they tend to ignore you. I also saw in that area a few barracudas swimming near the bottom of the sea.

As I left, I noticed a group of divers entering the ship's hull through a hatch. Intrigued by the prospect of exploring the vessel's interior and seeking the comfort of companionship, I decided to join them rather than venturing inside alone.

Upon entering the ship there was a kind of empty room which we crossed by and went down a long hallway, about 25-30 meters long. On both sides of this hall there were empty spaces with abundant small fish and a certain amount of natural light. I was glad I was wearing my gloves to avoid tripping and scratching myself when going through the hatches.

The truth is, I didn't stop long to look at each chamber from side to side, so as not to lose my rhythm and the divers I was following.

Being inside a ship of such dimensions triggered a lot of fascination for me and I thought how lucky I was to be observing and exploring these structures, in the depths of the ocean, which once served different functions other than entertaining divers. I couldn't help but imagine the stories of the sailors who had once been aboard. The beauty of the underwater world was truly magical.

After this long corridor, we exited one by one through a hatch, to the outside and there was our guide trying to gather his group of divers to begin the ascent.

We climbed slowly. I did it with that feeling of someone who does not want to leave and wants some more. I was holding onto the rope that connected us with the buoy on the surface, and from time to time I looked down, like saying goodbye to this extraordinary experience.

Being there was a wonderful experience, and I was sad not to have been able to see other areas of the ship. But it was time to return safely to the surface.

When doing a dive of this type, we must take precautions for the air we consume, so that it is sufficient for all stages of the ride, safety stops and any eventuality that may arise.

We make the first safety stop at 15 meters under the water surface, given that some or all the divers could have descended below 25 meters. We stopped for 3 minutes without any incident, while breathing normally to give the body the time necessary to eliminate the nitrogen bubbles.

As the group of divers held onto the rope and maintained normal breathing, the concentration of bubbles surrounding us created an atmosphere of tension. We persevered through this challenging environment for a seemingly endless three minutes during this safety stop.

We continued ascending then, until we reached 5 meters under the surface of the water. There we began our second safety stop.

As I checked my diving pressure gauge during this stop, I realized my air tank was nearly empty, leaving me with insufficient air to complete the mandatory 3-minute safety stop and continue my ascent.

Understanding the urgency of the situation, I knew I had to act quickly and rationally to find a solution. Surfacing immediately was not an option, as I still needed to complete the safety stop to allow for more nitrogen bubbles to dissipate from my body, despite the surface being tantalizingly close.

I decided to swim closer to our guide, signaling that my air supply was running low and showing him my pressure gauge. Recognizing the urgency of the situation, he promptly offered me his secondary regulator, which we all carry as a safety measure. I steadied myself and prepared for the crucial regulator exchange, knowing that every moment counted.

When changing the regulator, you must be careful not to open your mouth because you swallow water.

I removed my regulator from my mouth and closed my lips. The "new" regulator should be introduced in such a way that it enters the mouth slowly, with some resistance, but not opening your mouth.

As this regulator was inside my mouth, immediately, our guide pressed the purge button on the regulator, to eliminate any water that could have entered the system and my mouth, thus ensuring the supply of clean, unobstructed air.

After this incident, we completed the 3-minute safety stop and surfaced.

I thanked God for helping me overcome that contingency quickly and calmly and giving me the confidence that I could succeed. I also thanked my partner for sharing his air, at that critical moment.

It became evident that my estimation of air consumption and time spent exploring the ship had been significantly off. I had underestimated the demands of the dive, including the descent and ascent, which led to my tank running out of air. Fortunately, a fellow diver had sufficient air and graciously shared it with me.

In hindsight, I may have spent too much time exploring the vessel or perhaps my heightened emotions and excitement during the dive caused me to breathe more heavily, consuming air at a faster rate. Despite these challenges, the feeling of accomplishment upon reaching the surface was truly indescribable.

Undoubtedly, my years of training and accumulated experience played a crucial role in my ability to respond swiftly and decisively when faced with the critical situation of my air tank reaching a dangerously low level. Despite the urgency, I remained composed and focused, successfully communicating my situation to the guide and executing a proper regulator change, drawing upon the skills honed during my training courses.

Thankfully, I never experienced shortness of breath during the incident. My diligent monitoring of my equipment and timely checks of the pressure gauge allowed me to stay informed about my air supply and take appropriate action when necessary.

Apart from the intense experience I had on this dive and the learning acquired, I must mention that Spiegel Grove is truly a spectacular place for diving.

It is located at a safe enough depth for certified recreational divers and has managed to become a vibrant artificial reef, attracting a beautiful diversity of marine life. Corals, sponges, and tropical fish have made this place their habitat.

HILMA HOOKER AT BONAIRE

Another of my trips to visit shipwrecks was on the Island of Bonaire, which is located in the Caribbean Sea, off the western coast of Venezuela.

Diving on this island is something extremely spectacular. Not only because of its warm and calm waters, but because there are countless places to dive since the island is designed to attract tourists and especially scuba divers.

In the clear and pleasant waters of Bonaire there is a shipwreck that can be reached by walking from the shore, into shallow waters near the port of Kralendijk. This is the Hilma Hooker.

This shipwreck lies on one of its sides at about 27 meters. deep, but you can reach it at about 16 meters deep, on its opposite side.

The Hilma Hooker was a cargo transport built in the Netherlands in 1951, which generally sailed between Europe and Africa. However, in 1984, the Hilma Hooker was confiscated in Bonaire, by local authorities, due to alleged legal charges related to drug trafficking.

While anchored in the port of Bonaire, the ship sank under circumstances that are not entirely clear.

Over time this shipwreck has become a very popular site among divers in Bonaire, due to the great visibility and the possibility of exploring the structure of the shipwreck even inside.

Upon reaching the hull of the boat you can see the formations of sponges, corals and marine plants that have been growing there and therefore attract many small and medium-sized fish such as butterfly fish, angelfish, parrot fish, etc. On these reefs we saw a variety of brightly colored fish, including anthias and surgeonfish. Likewise, trumpet fish are abundant.

However, when I dived towards the side where this boat lies, about 25 meters down, barracudas were swimming, entering, and leaving the hull. Their sizes are intimidating, and I didn't even go near them.

On a tour of the exterior of this ship, I marveled at the immense propellers that once powered it. In this place there was a spectacular fauna. Countless fish came and went through the enormous propellers as if to snoop on the divers who were approaching it.

On my internal tour of the ship, I could see some empty spaces.

I entered what I imagined could have been a kitchen, because of some of the metal furniture and shelves that still existed, already eaten away by rust, and partially covered by coral. In another small room, I saw what could have been a bathroom.

I didn't see much more of this ship because I estimated that after being down there for about 30 minutes, my air reserve in my cylinder was enough to last nearly 10 more minutes, and I still had to make my safety stop during the ascent. Also, I had seen barracudas enter the boat earlier in the day, and I didn't want to run into any of them.

I consider my deep dives to explore shipwrecks to be for my enjoyment, and to get to see marine flora and fauna, in a calm way, without fears or stressful situations.

I really don't like having encounters with large fish (over five feet), because I don't know how I would handle such circumstances. Therefore, I prefer to avoid situations that can scare and stress me. Since I have not received the proper training to interact with large species, I prefer not to have close encounters with them.

I understand that, by having adequate training and learning to interact with marine fauna, you can fully enjoy new experiences, but this is not yet the case for me.

In short, visiting the Hilma Hooker was a refreshing experience; Seeing the diversity of marine flora and fauna, which has already formed on its hull and outside, made this underwater tour a fascinating dive.

THE GREAT ROQUE IN Puerto Cabello, Venezuela

In the waters of Puerto Cabello, in north Venezuela, at the Guabina Bay, there is a beautiful shipwreck called The Great Roque.

The Great Roque used to be tugboat, which was located in front of one of the main ports of Venezuela, Puerto Cabello, and because of its bad conditions, was threatening to sink any minute, and block and affect transit around this important port.

For this reason, in 2003 The Great Roque was sunk in a controlled manner, with the idea of creating a coral reef. Today, it is resting on its keel in the sands of this bay.

The wreck of The Great Roque was the first ship sunk in a voluntarily controlled manner in Venezuela.

This ship is nowadays a great popular attraction for divers, due to its large size and the fact that it is only 20 meters deep down the bottom of the sea.

The day we dived into this shipwreck the visibility was good and the water temperature was 24ºC

To visit this shipwreck, it was necessary to wear a full suit and gloves, which would provide protection for our hands and body.

Inside the hull we had to take certain precautions, identifying danger points.

Like any shipwreck, there are sharp pieces, due to the rust that has formed on the hull. Likewise, inside, we were careful to observe and avoid getting tangled with suspended objects such as cables and pipes from the ship itself, which are still present.

We found the engine room easily because it is exposed. Apparently, its roof came off violently with the explosion, during the controlled sinking.

I must day that the engine room is quite deteriorated, very rusty and it was difficult to detail its components.

Continuing the tour, we swam along a hallway that leads to a sort of dining room and some stairs that connect with other rooms.

This boat is so large that in a single dive it was not possible to see all its areas.

On our visit to its external part, we found that its hull still has some metal parts in good shape, although eaten away by rust. We saw railings, stairs leading to another level of the deck and metal structures that once served as supports for other structures, which already house several coral formations.

From the first moment we noticed that the local fauna has colonized the shipwreck and currently you can see a great variety of fish. We saw angelfish, conger eels, corocoros, guasa groupers, boxfish, parrotfish, pufferfish, surgeonfish, and unfortunately, there were several lionfish too. Throughout the area we saw corals of different varieties: brain corals, fire corals, anemones, moon corals and basket corals.

In conclusion, visiting The Great Roque was an extraordinary experience. Today this wreck is a vibrant reef; Marine life has colonized this ship in an impressive way.

THE SESOTRIS SHIP ON the coast of Isla Larga

In the waters of Puerto Cabello, Venezuela, specifically on Isla Larga, you can see part of this ship which is half-sunk.

The history of this ship dates to the Second World War, when this German merchant ship, which transported a variety of products between Venezuela and Europe, received orders to take refuge in Venezuela, given the war.

While in the waters of Puerto Cabello, in 1941, a mutiny arose on board, by its crew, who set it on fire, to prevent it from being seized and falling into the hands of the allied forces, during the war.

After the fire, the Sesostris was so destroyed that it was impossible to rebuild.

In consequence, by orders of the then president Isaías Medina Angarita, it was scrapped, then towed and abandoned on an island near Puerto Cabello called Isla Larga, where it sank. There it remains sunken, as a mute witness and memory of that sad episode.

Inside the Sesostris you can only see parts of the ship such as its mast, part of its stern and some corridors and rooms.

Today this wreck is an excellent site for diving, and especially for the practice and training of divers who want to start visiting sunken ships, mainly due to its location in shallow waters.

Although the visibility was not perfect in these waters, we managed to dive and visit some of its parts, such as some rooms and the huge engine room.

Everything was quite rusty, so we preferred to wear full suits and gloves.

It is impressive to see the marine diversity that lives there, both inside the hull and around it. There, we observed practically the same fauna and flora that we had seen on the shipwreck The Great Roque, since both shipwrecks are not far from each other.

Other Memorable Dives

B ONAIRE.
On this beautiful Island, which is part of the Netherlands, and it is located northwest of the Venezuelan coast, we did several dives during the day, at night, and to a shipwreck. It is worth mentioning one that I remember very especially, for the beauty of its marine ecosystem.

I am referring to diving at Salt Pier. This is a pier created for the extraction of sea salt. It's easy accessibility walking from the beach makes this site a popular destination for both, divers and underwater photographers.

The pillars of this pier, which is located at about 100 meters from the beach, underwater look like majestic works of living art. Its incrustations of colorful sponges and corals constitute a wonderful marine habitat. Large schools of fish congregate between the pillars and around as if they wanted to take refuge from the sun, under the shadows created by the pier.

As I approach these pillars, the fish, which abound in large numbers, remain calm and make way for you, but they do not leave the place.

I carefully took pictures of angelfish, tang fish, and a large school of butterflyfish hovering around the pier pillars and us, as if they did not care about our presence.

Given the unique structure of the Salt Pier, with its pillars and refuge areas, at only about only 7 meters deep, fish of various bright colors abound all year round.

There we could see several hole fish, such as gobies and blennies, that were hiding between the cracks in the pillars. A truly spectacular site!

Towards the deepest area of the place, there is an abundance of marine flora in which crustaceans hid. We were able to find a large turtle perched on the sand, which I approached to take photos and a video.

In the distance we also saw barracudas passing in small groups.

In these waters you can see vast number of trumpet fish, with their elongated bodies and tubular mouths, which mostly got across us slowly and fearlessly.

Towards the shore of the beach, almost getting to the end of my dive, at about four meters below the surface of the water, I saw in front of me a beautiful, medium-sized olive ridley turtle. As it was swimming, I followed it for a while, taking a video carefully, until it surfaced for some air.

The richness of the marine ecosystem in Bonaire is truly fascinating. Its flora and corals still retain those vibrant colors that characterize healthy ecosystems, and its fauna is impressively colorful and abundant.

CUBA.

Cuba offers a remarkable scuba diving experience with its unique underwater landscape. In addition to submerged boats, I encountered military relics such as tanks, light artillery, and even old Jeeps, still bearing their tires and steering wheels. These structures, now transformed into artificial reefs, have enriched the local marine ecosystem in a remarkable way.

In addition to these military remnants, Cuba is also home to well-planned, purpose-built structures designed to promote coral reef formation. These formations, along with the diverse marine life they attract, have created a captivating environment for divers to explore and appreciate the beauty and complexity of the underwater world.

Furthermore, I have come across purposefully built structures designed to promote coral reef formation beyond just underwater tourism. These well-planned and visually striking sites, teeming with diverse marine life, showcase the beauty of the underwater world and the importance of preserving it for generations to come.

NEPTUNE MEMORIAL REEF

In South Florida, an extraordinary underwater realm known as the Neptune Memorial Reef can be found just 3 nautical miles east of Key Biscayne, at a depth of approximately 7 meters. Spanning an impressive 16 acres of the seafloor, this starfish-shaped artificial reef is a sight to behold.

During my dive, I was fortunate enough to explore a collection of beautifully designed concrete structures created to stimulate coral growth and provide a thriving habitat for diverse marine life. Each structure has been thoughtfully crafted to contribute to the overall health of the ecosystem while also showcasing its aesthetic appeal.

One of the most striking features of the Neptune Memorial Reef is a large pergola adorned with numerous arch-like entrances. The site also boasts a magnificent stone lion, which serves as a popular spot for divers to capture memorable selfies.

Another eye-catching element is a tall pedestal bearing an Aztec calendar, nestled beneath yet another pergola. Smaller figures can be found scattered throughout the area, adding further intrigue and charm to this underwater sanctuary.

Interestingly, the Neptune Memorial Reef serves as an underwater cemetery, providing a final resting place for individuals who have chosen cremation.

Divers can observe metal plates on the seafloor, inscribed with the names of those who have been laid to rest within this tranquil marine haven.

Over time, a variety of corals, sponges, and plants have taken root among the structures, enhancing the site's allure, and fostering an active, dynamic habitat. This vibrant ecosystem attracts a multitude of marine species, including a kaleidoscope of fish that delight divers with their colorful presence.

Given its undeniable beauty, shallow depth, and exceptional luminosity, the Neptune Memorial Reef has become a sought-after destination for divers seeking an unforgettable experience.

As a testament to the delicate balance between human creativity and the resilience of nature, this remarkable site stands as a true marvel beneath the waves.

Final Notes

Without doubt, obtaining proper certification is essential to embarking on recreational diving. This certification process not only ensures your safety but also opens up a world of opportunities for exploring the depths of the sea, regardless of your location. Most certifications are internationally recognized, allowing divers to embark on underwater adventures across the globe.

Furthermore, engaging in scuba diving under the guidance of an experienced instructor is crucial, especially for beginners. Building trust with your instructor and heeding their advice can significantly enhance your diving experience, as they possess invaluable knowledge about the underwater environment and its potential challenges. Their expertise will inform you about safe diving practices, such as determining when it is safe to descend, how long you should spend underwater, and the importance of safety stops.

As you become more experienced, diving with a companion is highly recommended. Even when you are no longer a novice, it is essential never to dive alone. A diving partner can provide assistance in unforeseen situations and help ensure your safety throughout the dive.

Moreover, sharing your diving experiences with a companion not only adds an element of camaraderie but also enhances overall safety during your underwater adventures. By prioritizing safety and collaboration, you can fully immerse yourself in the wonders of the underwater world while creating lasting memories with fellow diving enthusiasts.

Another important recommendation is to respect the interval times, after diving and before flying. It is necessary to give our body a chance to get used to the change in atmospheric pressure once we get to the surface.

The change in atmospheric pressure when flying after a dive increases the risk of decompression sickness due to the additional reduction in atmospheric pressure when you are flying.

Therefore, to minimize the risk of decompression sickness, it is important to allow sufficient time between diving and flying. For non-decompression dives, it is recommended to wait at least 12 hours before boarding a plane. However, if you have completed multiple dives over several days, it is advisable to extend this interval to 18 hours. In the case of deep dives involving decompression, a minimum of 24 hours should elapse before flying to ensure your body has adequate time to adjust and avoid potential health complications.

Epilogue

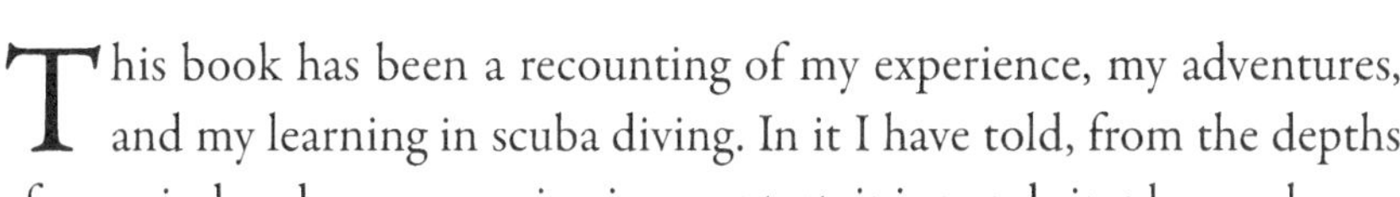

This book has been a recounting of my experience, my adventures, and my learning in scuba diving. In it I have told, from the depths of my mind and my memories, in an entertaining and simple way, how a childhood dream managed to come true.

My determination to satisfy that curiosity of learning about the marine life and its depths finally led me, during my adult years, not only to immerse myself in that wonderful world of the blue, but also to enjoy it intensely.

All this experience allowed me to become more aware of the marine ecosystem and the importance of contributing to its conservation. Likewise, I learned to manage my fears with logic and serenity, and to establish a more intimate relationship with the beauties of our beautiful underwater world.

Writing this book has given me the great satisfaction of reliving unforgettable moments of my life as a scuba diver.

It has been a constant exercise of bringing memories into the paper and evoking emotions again. Despite my age, I remember the places, the people, the teachings, the emotions, and the experiences lived in a palpable way, which is why I have captured them here, with honesty and great enthusiasm.

I still feel that spark of adventure that ignites my passion for exploration urging me to venture forth to new horizons as long as God and good health allow me to do so.

! I hope you have enjoyed this reading!

Illustration Link

If you want to see photo illustrations or videos about my stories, they are available on my INSTAGRAM channel.

To access my Instagram channel you must scan, with a cell phone, the following QR code:

@MIS_AVENTURAS_SUBMARINAS

OR CLICK: https://bit.ly/3JNPKqM

About the Author

Leonor Osorio Granado was born in Caracas, Venezuela where she lived and studied until the end of her teenage years. She completed her higher education in the United States in the area of Urban Planning, at East Carolina University, and obtained a Master's degree in Urban Transit Planning, at the University of Tennessee, Knoxville, where she married in 1980, and had two daughters: Ailyn and Aldys

She practiced her professional life mostly in Venezuela for over 20 years and later worked in a few other countries for 10 more years. She speaks 3 languages.

Her main hobby is and has been scuba diving, which she enjoys frequently since the year 2000. By practicing this sport, she has obtained several PADI Certifications, with which she has been able to fulfill her dream of exploring and enjoying the underwater world, in different parts of the American continent.

Currently, she has retired from her professional life, and she works as a Medical Interpreter in English, Spanish and Portuguese, for patients in the Seattle, Washington area. She is also the author of "El Mar y Yo, Relatos de mis Aventuras en el Fondo Marino" (Spanish Edition).

Don't miss out!

Visit the website below and you can sign up to receive emails whenever LEONOR OSORIO GRANADO publishes a new book. There's no charge and no obligation.

https://books2read.com/r/B-A-ZUGHB-BFQBD

BOOKS 2 READ

Connecting independent readers to independent writers.

www.ingramcontent.com/pod-product-compliance
Lightning Source LLC
Chambersburg PA
CBHW050606160726
48003CB00003B/1065